We never know when the journey will call to
us, but we all must remember one thing,
Memento Mori. We must live this life as well
as we can. We must take the chances and risk
the rewards of a subtle life, because we were
not made for the normalcy it brings. Take your
heart out, and free it. This book is for the
moments we make, for those who make it all
worth it by taking a break from sitting and
staring at others live a life you wish you could.
You deserve it, too.

-karnes-

# JFK to Utah

## -A Poet's Journey-

10:58AM          10.11.23          J21 Delta Flight

Today is Asa's birthday. Number 36 for him. It is amazing how quickly all of these years have gone by. It feels like only the other day he and I were outside at Mom's house, playing 1 on 1 basketball games until almost dark and out mother was calling us in for dinner. it is hard to pinpoint ideas while traveling and not being able to write when you feel the need to, or ever remember what it was you were trying to write in the first place. Yesterday flew by quickly, as did the entire trip. It felt as though we were waiting a month or more for this trip top happen, and now, we are already flying back to SLC. We got up this morning at 5AM. We basically ate and snacked all day yesterday. We watched the news on CNN from the time we got out food until 10PM. The coverage of Israel and Gaza has been nonstop. Last night was the first time we actually had a tv with Americans speaking on it since the second of this month. We did not watch tv at all except at the first house in Careno, but that was only Netflix, The Lincoln Lawyer. We were in bed and asleep by 10:30PM. We got up at five, and we were already packed for the most part. We got everything ready but I forgot my sweatpants. We caught the elevator down to the lobby, walked through the entrance, and finally found the escalator to go up to our Terminal, which was Terminal 1. It took us a little bit to find the security check to use, but we found it after getting through the passport check and the luggage and personal check. Asa thought he had lost his wallet and passport, and experienced a brief panic attack as we all did. The agents working there were not helpful at all. Super lazy and not a lot of English being spoken. He found both of them at the bottom of the second bin he used for his possessions. There was a couple next to us who were laughing, because the husband said, "It is usually me." Meaning it always happens to him. Everything else went rather smoothly, but the walk to the actual gate was a fucking haul. It took at least twenty minutes to get there,. I was sweating by the time we found the gate and sat down with all of our bags. We arrived around 6:15AM or so, and well before the 9AM flight and 8AM check-in. I did some journaling a little while after I got settled in. I bought a smoothie, some juice, and a Pellegrina water. I watched the gate area fill up with more and more people, and hit max capacity around 7:30AM. I went to get another bottle of water, and as I was standing in line, there was this guy from New York, his mom, and siblings, asking the cashier all kinds of questions. I felt bad for the woman, because he wads being such a dick to her, making her answer questions she did not know and changing his food order several times. Then they left and a blonde woman was next. She ordered a cappuccino and two drinks, with a blueberry muffin,. She was having issues working the credit card machine. She finally got it worked out and I was able yo get my waters and head back. We started getting in line yo board at 8:30AM.

There was already a substantial line formed, which was funny to me because the ones who are usually standing are the ones in the back of the place. we got upgraded thanks to Asa making it happen. We would have been in the back like the first time with no leg and arm room, all squeezed and packed in like sardines. We got to move up to Sky Class, which has more leg room, better service, more food choices, and an overall healthier experience. As we got checked in, I was "randomly" selected for a baggage and personal check. I had to go behind the walkway where they did not even check my bag. I had to remove my shoes, and they swabbed my hands for sickness or drugs I assumed. It took less than ten minutes, but it was annoying nonetheless. I got seated and met Phil. We hit it off immediately. He was super chill with a peaceful candor. He is from the Bronx originally and lived in Italy for five years from the ages of eight to thirteen. He lived with his dad until his father passed away last November. His parents split when he was young and his mother moved back to Italy where she was born in Como. He was visiting her and his sister this trip for three weeks. He is probably going to move back in April he said. He still has a lot to do in order to move there permanently. He is divorced and has been split-up for over nine years. We talked about the whole trip I had and showed him photos of it. We actually took the same photo in Bellagio. I showed him photos of my time in the military, because his first instinct was to think I was in the Marines because of the tattoos.

We ended up talking for around four hours or close to it. We were told by one of the flight attendants to not talk or at least not to be as loud. People were trying to sleep, which is ridiculous, but we kept talking anyway. I was able to get a few photos of the Alps this time. It is such a majestic view looking down at those monuments of the world. We were in the air and flying a little after 9AM. Flying out of Milan, going through Turin, Geneva, Sens, just south of Paris, Argentan, Saint Helier, and now over the Celtic Sea. We will be flying over the Atlantic Sea in a few hours. While I was watching the news last night, I thought we might have a few passengers on board today from Israel trying to flee the country for safety or return back to their homes in the states. We have a family on here it turns out. A mother, two sisters, and their father. The sister wanted to go sit with her dad, but the flight attendant was not having it. It was such a scene and ordeal. The mother was crying and arguing. The daughter was crying, but they would not let the girl change seats. The mother then began talking to us a after it all went down. I felt horrible for both mother and daughter. They have been on the run for the last few days. You can tell they have been through it by the look on their faces and the energy they had about them. The mother was irate, screaming almost, telling the flight attendant, "You have not been on the run, sleeping in your shoes, hearing the sirens, hearing the rockets." The mother is asleep now, and the daughter is listening to music on her iPad. I am going to write something for her and give it to her when we land. I am still trying to think of what to write, but I know it will come to me. My pen just ran out of ink. Luckily, I brought two more pens with me. We still have four hours and thirty-eight minutes left before we land. I am going to write the two writings, one for Phil and one for the daughter in front of me. It really is a wild concept when flying. You board a plane full of strangers and the randomness doesn't stop when you sit down. I have only flown a few times where the person sitting next to me did not say a word the entire flight. I find it a common theme in my life, where strangers come up to me out of the blue and talk to me as if they have known me since we were kids. If it isn't an in depth conversation, there is still small talk to pass the time. Everywhere I have gone throughout my life, this has happened to some degree. I find comfort in it, because I haven't always felt comfortable around myself, but people come up to me and tell me my eyes look familiar, and then after that, the talking only stops once one of us has to leave or go somewhere else in our travels. I will write in here again when we land and get through customs.

4:19PM       10.11.23       Lake Michigan

We landed ahead of schedule. I finished writing the two writings for Phil and Dara. I took a break afterwards and watched Guardians of the Galaxy Vol.3. It was the best one of the series by far and a perfect ending for the trilogy. Phil kept waking up and going to sleep throughout the rest of the flight. The food they served was exceptional. The started with a crepe apple(toasted like apple pie), then they served a creme brulee and calzone, which I did not eat, but everything was amazing. The crew who worked the flight were phenomenal. They always made sure we had what we needed, and were probably the best flight crew I have ever been a part of. I watched Antman & Wasp Quantamania as well. It was not the best, but I wanted to watch it regardless of what others had said about it. I fast forwarded half of it, but the ending was pretty good at least. We landed around 11:30AM or so I think, I was able to give the writing to Dara before we got off the flight. She cried, as did her mother when she began reading it. I hope the next chapter of her life is beautiful and peaceful. I told her that as well as her mother. Phil and I parted ways, as I gave him his writing and said goodbye. We got to customs, which was not as bad as I thought it would be, but it still took around forty-five minutes to get through all of it. Then we had to re-check our bags and go through another security check. They pulled my bag because of my typewriter.

It happened to me twice this entire trip. They took it out of my bag and sent it through the x-ray. It is so fucking annoying that a machine from the 60's gets pulled without an electronic mechanism within it. That added an extra fifteen minutes of building frustration for me. I just wanted coffee, and it seemed like they were fucking with me just because. We found the way to the gate and sat our bags down. I got dad and I two waters and ordered a Dunkin' Donuts coffee. I felt so relieved and thankful to be back in the States. I was telling Asa I did not take these privileges we have here for granted, but you do get used to them and they become so normal and a part of your everyday life. You forget how simple life is here until you force yourself to leave the country and see how ridiculous life really can be. The coffee was nothing close to Nesso coffee, but it was what I needed. Asa ordered a birthday beer at the bar, which was well deserved. I hate how we were stuck flying for thirteen hours today instead of celebrating his birthday as we should have. I told him we would celebrate tomorrow or the next day. The two bottles of water were nearly twelve dollars. The coffee was just under five dollars for maybe twelve ounces. The prices are the prices, but again, just fucking happy to be home in the States. I kept thinking it was later than it was. By the time I finished the coffee, it was not even 2PM. Before I finished drinking it, a black woman came up to me just as I had took out my typewriter and was finishing my first page, and onto the second. She heard the typing, turned around, and asked me,

"They still make those things?" I laughed and said, yes. I asked how much time she had to give me. She said ten minutes. She had thought I asked if she wanted to type something, but she finally got the hint that I was going to type her something. I said give me two minutes and I will have it ready for you. She looked on in amazement the entire time I was typing. I finished it before three minutes were up. She asked for a photo of it with me and her, and said she would post if on the Delta Facebook page. I am not sure I will ever see it, the writing or her ever again, but I do hope the writing helps her. Her name was Melissa Precious. It was the first time I had ever done that before, so it was really sensational and such a riveting feeling typing on the spot for someone. I finished the other writing I was doing before she stopped by, then I went over to Shake Shack, which was right next to us. I got myself a chicken sandwich and bought Asa some fries and a Shake-burger. We boarded about an hour later. It is a full flight and we should land within two hours and thirty-five minutes. I will write more once I get to Asa's place.

3:26PM                10.12.23                SLC

We landed in Salt Lake City around 7:30PM and went to the seven eleven by Asa's house to grab snacks to eat before bed since it was late getting to the house. When we landed. it was forty-four degrees and raining. We got unpacked and watched the LA Dodgers vs Arizona Diamondbacks game three of the ALDS. Arizona won four to two, and swept the Dodgers after they had won one hundred plus games again for the third straight season in a row. Asa and dad fell asleep on the couch before the game ended. Asa had kept the air mattress blown up so he slept there and dad slept on the couch. I slept in Asa's bed. I do not remember falling asleep. I wore a eye-mask the flight crew gave us earlier in the day, and it worked perfectly. We got up around 8AM, made coffee, and I had four cups. It felt amazing waking up in the States and having coffee without needing to go out to get it at a cafe. We went into town around 12PM to Smith's to grab some groceries. Asa made potato soup, which was bought at Trader Joe's. All you had to do was put it in a pot and heat it up. It was still in the forties and raining when we got up. The leaves here have all changed over. A true fall day here in Salt Lake City. We got back and ate the soup. All three of us had two bowls each. We watched College Gameday Scoreboard, then The Pat McAfee Show on ESPN2. Now, we are watching The Lincoln Lawyer season two on Netflix. It is a nice, peaceful, and relaxing day here. I will not be doing too much here until we leave next week. Slow and easy days til then. The weather is supposed to be better tomorrow all the way until we leave next Monday or Tuesday. We hope to get on a flight by then since we are doing stand by. I am not really worried about it, because I know what is meant to happen, will. It will take some time getting used to being here again after being in Italy and in a part of the world that would not classify as actual civilization. I know I am ready to be out of Texas. This trip did not change my mind. It only strengthened it. I know it will happen. I am going to do whatever it takes to get my life back and get back out into the real world. I cannot continue being a caretaker for my father. I am wasting away here and missing out on years of my life by doing so. I just need to be patient and understand everything happens for a reason. We must take it one day at a time and do one thing at a time. It does not do anyone any good jumping days in order to get to where you want to be or bypassing memories you would miss out by enjoying the now as it is presently. I will drink my coffee today, look at the mountains, and become them when the time comes.

11:37AM          10.14.23          SLC

After a few days of being back in the States, my mind, body, and soul are still trying to readjust back to this timezone, sleep schedule, and just being here in general. I have not had jet-lag either trip to or back from Italy. After sleeping for nine hours on Thursday, we did not do too much. We went to the grocery store and got some things that have lasted until yesterday. We watched College Football and the NFL Thursday night game. The chiefs won against the Broncos, nineteen to eight. Boring game if I am being honest. We watched the Phillies win and the Diamondbacks win. I went to bed around 10PM and slept in again a bit until 8AM. We walked to Park Cafe and ate the first real breakfast in about three days. I had granola, bananas, yogurt bowl, with two scrambled eggs, and three cups of coffee. After that, we walked back to the house and watched some tv until we got ready and Asa drove us to Park City, which is around thirty minutes from Salt Lake City. The leaves have changed again today, with a fresh dusting of snow on the mountains here. It feels superb driving on American roads. Asa took us to the No Name Saloon bar and grill. I had a turkey burger, which was insanely good with homemade chips and salsa. We walked down Main street, all the way up and all the way down. we went to a coffee ship called, Atticus. Asa had said it would be a place I would enjoy, which he was correct. I got an

Americano and walked around in the shop. It was all decorated in Halloween decor and the vibe there was something I would definitely drive to and enjoy if I lived here. We walked the streets, which were packed with travelers, tourists, and locals. It was colder there. Somewhere in the fifties, but the wind chill was fifteen degrees cooler than that. We stayed there for almost two hours, then left around 2:45PM. We drove to the outlet stores a little further down the road to the Under Armor shop, where I bought some cheap running shoes since I did not bring any with me for the trip. I met a guy there who helped check me out. We talked about the Military service. He served in the Law Enforcement in Miami Dade County fir fifteen years, then served two years for a special unit for human trafficking. He took off an extra fifty percent off my purchase to go along with the forty percent sale they were running for some of the products. It ended up being twenty-five dollars for some decent running shoes. By far the cheapest shoes I have bought since probably college. I wanted a different pair, but they did have my size. We made it back to Salt Lake City before 4PM. We ended up going back to Smith's to get more groceries and made it back to the house around 4:30PM. Groceries are definitely more expensive here than in Italy. It is such a farce, a kick in the nuts for those of us who work our asses off only to spend half or two weeks worth of pay on a couple bags of groceries. In Italy, you can buy thirty pounds of groceries for less than thirty dollars. We unpacked the bags and were settled into the night by 6PM. I showered early, and we were watching College Football by then. Tulane versus Memphis. Tulane won, then Stanford began playing Colorado. The Buffs were up twenty-nine to zero at halftime, and Asa was asleep on the couch by 8PM. Dad was still up and I was not tired, but I knew Asa needed to sleep. I was getting up at 630AM to run. I found out this morning after working out that Colorado lost to Stanford in double overtime, forty-six to forty-three. Brutal lost for Deion and his kids, I got up at 630AM, got dressed and ready to go by 640AM. It was forty-three degrees when I got outside. Asa let me borrow some running pants, hoodie, and socks. The UA shoes were not the best, but I did not need the best for the next few days. I just needed something besides my Danner boots. I walked about a mile or so down the street, caught a photo of Jupiter, and walked East to where the park is. I got on the trail and started running. There were not a lot people out there besides the homeless walking around, trying to get warm. The running trail is super nice and laid out perfectly with wood shavings or mulch to help the knees and ankles when running. It is also a trail for owners and their dogs. One lap is 2.2 miles. I began seeing the sun come up. I have missed these sunrise colors so much here in Utah. I have not seen any that come close while being in the States, but Arizona comes close. After the second lap, a few more people started showing up. The colors intensified every half lap and I was able to catch some pretty gnarly photos of them.

It felt really odd running again. Sea legs, and it almost felt like I was learning how to run again. I have never took that much time off from working out. I hate being this behind on my health, but I got it done and ended up doing over six miles. I ran down the end of the street to capture a few more sunrise photos. Crisp. Clean. Refreshing. Vibrant. Intense. Serene. Magical. I am almost certain I was the only one out there taking photos. I was like that in St. George, always snapping photos, as if I had not already lived there for half a year already. It never gets old for me, because each one is a different, a new color added, a new color thrown out, clouds adjacent or barely hanging onto the sky. There is never the same sunrise or sunset that is the same, which is why it is all the more meaningful to me. I got back to Asa's around 8AM. Almost an hour and a half run. I had four cups of coffee, then watched College Gameday. Asa has chicken going and dad is helping him with the grill. The lunar eclipse is today. It is the first one since 2017. Carpe Diem. It is a beautiful day to live. it is a beautiful day to be here in Utah, living a dream I will continue living even after I find my way back to this place.

11:49AM                    10.15.23                    SLC

We watched College Football all day long. Asa had the chicken ready, rice, veggies, peppers, chips and dips all set out and ready to go a little after the first game came on. It was another beautiful day here in Salt Lake City. High in the sixties, sunny, and clear. I sat down on the couch all day and enjoyed the company of my dad and brother, we snacked on and off half of the day, We ended up staying yup until 1030PM or so. Being here, I can just feel the energy balanced, even though I still have some anxiety about not knowing what to do when I get back to Texas, with dad not having a job and no vehicle. It is not easy on my mind and body, holding in all of that built up and pent up energy. I do not want to be in Texas anymore at all. I do not want to be in Portland. I am tired of behind the son who sacrifices for the betterment of someone else. The only few positives from it are me being able to save up money for whatever I do decide to do after the end of this year. Before you know it, it will be Thanksgiving, Christmas, then New Year's Eve. Getting back to this part of the adventure, I have enjoyed it fully, made some sales on the website since being away, and feel good with how that side of my life is going. It has been weird for me not creating items to add to my website to make money, but I plan on doing a few more books this year, a few with less pages made from the poetry and memories I have made since being in Italy and everywhere in-between. This morning, I got up at 7AM without an alarm, got dressed and was at the park by 715AM. I went a different way than yesterday. It was not as cold, but it was still in the forties. It was clear as ever, so not the best sunrise, but there were just enough clouds to add the reds and pinks. I ended you by the seven eleven, which is close to Asa's house. It is a landmark for me to use when I am out running and a tool to gauge the direction needed to get back. I was only out there for an hour and ran three laps. A lot more homeless out there this morning, and more people in general. I finished the last lap and went back the same way I came, I thought. I ended up going south to the downtown portion, and eventually ran an entire lap around the surrounding area. I was trying to find the Park Cafe, which is less than a mile from where Asa lives. I looked up his address and finally found my way back after taking a few sunrise shots of the mountains. I got back around 8AM. Asa and dad were watching the London NFL game, Baltimore versus Titans, and a fresh pot of coffee was made. I burned almost eight hundred calories within the hour I was out there, I had one cup of coffee, then Asa drove to the Bagel Project and got us bagels. I had a raisin bagel with strawberry jam and cream cheese, and orange juice. I ended up drinking three more cups of coffee, and managed to finally to an Instagram post. I always find it easier to write more introspectively and with a broader outlook being out and about. It had me thinking about life and where I want to be, what I want to do, and always makes me feel better being able to stay active and get a morning workout in, I am not sure when we are leaving. Maybe tomorrow or Tuesday, but I know I am ready to get out of Texas. NFL all day today. A peaceful, easy Sunday. Carpe Diem. You deserve happiness. I know one day it will find you and it will be because of the effort you have put into it. We are never ready for change, but when it comes to us as our reward, I hope you take it in and embrace it fully. There is only so much you can do while you are in this situation, but do not go around blaming yourself for how it is today. You did not cost your father his job. You did not make your father spend all of his money, when he should have saved some of it for this stage of his life. You are not the reason why things are this way. Do what you feel like you need to without feeling remorseful for it or feeling guilty for living your life. Stop giving other people power over you. If you feel the energy is not reciprocated, exit and leave them out of your life for good. They only come around when they need something. The quicker you realize that, the better off you will be. The same goes for love. Once it is ready to find you, you will have exactly what you have always needed. You will be ready for it when the day is ready to grant you with such a beautiful gift. Until then, focus on your work, on your writing, and put out the material you believe in. Trust your instincts and intuition more. Believe in your fate.

4:56PM            10.16.23            SLC

We began watching NFL as soon as the RedZone channel started. I do not remember leaving the couch other than going to the bathroom and getting more of my drinks. Asa ordered us Firehouse Subs. He and I had the Philly cheese-steak and dad got the turkey. Asa's ex came over last night a little before 10PM. She was super nice, sweet, and a flight attendant herself. She stayed for about an hour. We watched the Bills versus Giants, and she left fifteen minutes after the game had ended. Dad and I went to bed. Asa got to bed around 12AM. I did not get up until after 8AM. My body needed to rest after exerting myself more in the last two days than I had previously in the two weeks prior. I got to sleep sometime after 11AM. I got plenty of rest to feel good, but I know my body is still recovering from the trip. I had coffee, watched GetUP!, Pat McAfee show, then we went into the downtown area of Salt Lake City. We ate at Red Rock. I had chicken tacos. Asa and dad had the fish and chips. We left there and Asa drove us to Alta. It was around forty-five minutes away to get to where he wanted to show us in order to send out his drone. The drive there was tremendous. Bright and full fall colors everywhere. The mountains. The snow. The vibe. The energy. I am not sure of the elevation, but it felt high enough to where it was fifteen degrees cooler, and it was not even near the top of the slopes. We stayed there for about thirty minutes and then began driving back. On the way down, I felt a panic attack coming on. I am sure it was the half of can of Red Bull I drank prior, but I felt trapped and suffocated being in-between mountains and feeling out of control by my own place within it all. It finally went away and we went to Smith's to get more groceries. Asa went to Trader Joe's to get things for dinner. He made filet steaks, mashed potatoes, and a few other things. I typed for an hour and finished with some of the single pages I had brought with me for the trip to Italy I did not get a chance to use. Dallas plays the Chargers tonight. We will see how it all goes. Carpe Diem.

8:11AM          10.17.23     SLC     Cleveland St.

Yesterday was incredible. After we got back from the store with the groceries, Asa had to go back into town for charcoal. He grilled filet mignon, made asparagus, mashed potatoes with a garlic sauce. It was absolutely top shelf cooking. He has done so well for himself here. I am so proud of the life he has fought for and carved out for himself. From the job he has, to the place he stays, to the way his life is, it is everything and more than I could have hoped for him after escaping our childhood and overcoming everything we had to. The deck was stacked against us but we have both prevailed. Even if I am still in Portland, at least he got away on his own. Dallas won last night, twenty to seventeen. It was about as ugly as a football game can be. Micha Parsons got a sack to make it third and ten with less than a minute left, then Gilly got an interception to end the game. Landry formation, victory formation. Dallas is 4-2 heading into their bye week. We went to bed around 10PM. Everyone seemed pretty tired and still trying to readjust being back here, I know my body is finally feeling good again. I have been thankful to have worked out several days being here. Saturday, Sunday, and today, After taking yesterday off, I slept fairly well overall. The day before leaving for somewhere, I always seem yo be restless, but I feel rested and ready for the trip today. I got up at 715AM, got dressed, and was outside by 730AM. I went down Cleveland Street and made the left towards, The Park Cafe, where the park is. The sunrise this morning was spectacular. It was showing off on our last day here. I have missed Utah so fucking much, simply because of the energy here. Above and below. It is the most tangible sensation I have felt. I ran one and a half laps and watched the sun rise over the mountains. There were quite a few people out there today, which is always beautiful to see. I continued taking pictures until I got back to Asa's place. There was this woman on the hill doing yoga, staring into the mountains. Serene. I am having coffee now, second cup, watching GetUp! I saw a squirrel and it looked right at me. It got as close as it could before running back into the tree. I remember being a kid in Clinton, New York, my mother would hand feed the chipmunks in the morning during the winter season. They would come onto the porch and you could hold out a whole peanut and it would take it right from your hands. Memories like that come back to me when I find myself in a similar place. It is easily one of my favorite memories as a child living up north, along with playing in the snow with my brothers. I will see you again, Utah.

10.17.23                9:23AM                SLC

She is not worried about being

too much. She knows the oceans too well

to concern herself with a few drops of

rain. To find out who you are, you will have

to lose everything you have ever loved. It is

only when a heart shatters do we find

the rest of who we were meant to be.

9:34AM                 10.17.23                 SLC

Today has been the most perfect day. It is the warmest

it has been. Not a single cloud in the sky. It is the day

of love and we have become it. Beginning and ending,

the song of solitude becomes a comforting solace

within the sun and stars. You are here for experience,

to learn before you approach the known. Every bit of

me is trying to piece together the pieces of the fallen,

the barren trees living within me. I am not here for

normalcies. There is no time for the next thing, for a

possible encounter. There is only today that is being

determined by what you do not do.

10:09AM                    10.17.23                    SLC

I wish there was a way to be closer to you while I was away. I wish there was more of me to give, but maxing out my love for more than one has been tiring. I am here with you. Some days, it is too much for me, giving to myself to you and to those in your life. I do not know if we will work, but it is not because we are not trying. Changes are never easy. They usually come out of nowhere, at a time you cannot express. They find you when you think you are ready. You are the universe, and within it all, chaos wraps its arms and legs around you, dearly holding onto the last thing it can love. Do not regret what you once loved, what you once thought would work. Everything is based on the now. Be prepared to fail, but also prepare yourself for the miracle you will become for someone else.

11:17AM                10.17.23                SLC

I get into these zones where I could write for hours,

days, nights at a time. My tiredness is not based on

anything but my inability to rest comfortably in

someone else's space. Take me to the moon and

beyond. Be there in your totality, and share your truths

with those who appreciate you. Anything else is a

waste of your life. Sunlight beckons to be touched in

a moment of unsettled magic. We are the act of life,

so whatever comes our way, be a youthful surprise of

uncharted love. Maybe down the road there will be less

signs and more awareness between the soul and body.

My heart at times ends up in my head, a beating

of madness ensues.

11:33AM                    10.17.23                    SLC

I may not get everything right all of the time, but I have tried my best to give myself love and attention. I have given way too many humans the best of me without giving myself any of it. Today, I chose myself. I may never understand why I have so much love to give, but never to the right person. Maybe they were all right for me and the journey I was on then and now. I am tired of writing about what I do not have, but I will never give up on love. It is not always going to be easy, this life, this love. We will never fully understand this pain, this loss. To understand what you do not know, you have to ask the questions and be prepared to be annihilated by the answers you find. To become love, you must first have it for yourself.

# *Never*

# *Before*

# *Seen*

# *Writings*

## CAPTION WRITING FROM 2022

I hope you never hold onto what is not meant for you. You will miss out on everything that is. Absence is how we value who we are. It is the unfolding of arms and embracing an idea, a feeling, a forgotten nostalgic sensation of your favorite memory. It is protecting your space against unwanted light and iridescent conflict. Do not lower yourself to meet those who do not stand up for who you are, for those who only sit when you are crying out for help that never comes. I have shed a million tears this year already. Some of them came from a place I rarely visit. It takes all of my energy to summon myself back to where I belong physically and mentally when I stay there too long mourning what has perished along the way. Sometimes, my self-awareness takes me out of everyone's life I am in. My conscious becomes a devilish tune only darkness can sing along to. Silhouettes rest above my head, swinging side to side like some ghost-like chandelier, reflecting and refracting what is no longer there. I have been pushed off a mountain top which took me years to climb. I looked back on my way down and it was me who sacrificed myself to get back to the front a line I created. To know yourself, you must value each voice inside of you. The one we hear, the one others hear, and the one nobody else can. It takes practice each day to enliven your own path, to garden your fields and enrich what has come to pass. I have met a million humans in my lifetime. Each one had a piece of someone else attached to them. You could tell where their markers were. Age twenty became a breaking point for some. Age fifty was when they found purpose. Some were near seventy and in love for the first time. I believe in connection, in a world where we are all tied to the same string. The frequency may change, but our connectivity remains a mirrored wave of up and downs. We meet who we need at the exact time and never a second sooner. There is no such thing as being late when it comes to living. Whether you end up finding out who you love or who loves you later on, everything leading up to that moment remains relevant to your journey. My deep thoughts will not stop digging. I have a thousand more shovels to use. I have a new earth to uncover with my hands or whatever tool I can find. Deep within this crust of warmth and coldness, I find myself burning alive, frostbitten, and barely hanging on, but I am living by detaching myself from the torture others wish upon me.

12:45PM                2.18.22                Texas

I have been back for a few days now. Each day

that has passed, has given me a new breath.

Ideas and words flood me. I am trying to

stay above the water's edge.

Love is the same thing.

4:37PM                 2.21.22                 Southlake

Not all days are the same for me.

I know that is an obvious statement

for a lot of us, but there was a stretch

when I did not have anything good to

think of in years. Slowly, I am crawling back

to the body I left behind when I was told

I would need to change to fit into a life

I was never meant to be a part of.

4:44PM			Nekter			Southlake


Money only seems to exist in these places.

I cannot remember going out before and

worrying about it being a burden. I will

never need a lot to be happy or whole,

but I will sacrifice to have what I need.

6:03PM               2.28.22          Cambria SL TX

Take time with yourself. Be prepared to sit

in silence and learn your breaths better.

Everyone is always in such a rush these

days that we forget how to care for who

we are. If you do not, no one will ever

fucking care to help you with what you

are dealing with. Humans are as selfish as

they have been taught to be when it comes

to their own needs over someone else's.

2:11PM　　　　3.6.24　　　　Texas

Looking back at when you left, I forgot how much of you became my life as the foundation gave way to my emptiness. I do not know why I offered you as much as I did when you only had your hands out for me to guess what was inside of one when you got tired of the mundane in your life. There were options for me, for you, for us, but you relied on your runaway tactics to make sure you ended up without me. I remember my days of running away, and how often I could never find myself regardless of where and how long I looked. I was too good at it, and I never thought in my lifetime I would meet someone who was better at it than I was, then turn around and use it against me in a way I was never prepared for. When we become the betrayal, leave everything you have learned behind.

12:30PM          5.24.19          St. George, UT

Then I woke up one day, and all I knew was her. All I knew were her sounds, her silence, her magic. All I knew was that I would give my last breath to a woman who gave me my lungs reason to never quit. A woman who gave my heart reason to speak. A woman who gave my soul light. All I know is her, and it is fucking glorious. May we all find someone to help us when we feel helpless by trying to do it all on our own. We may fail, but failing is only a negative thing when you give up the second time.

11:11AM                5.23.19              St. George, UT

Eleven eleven has a new meaning because of you. It used to mean just being in sync with the universe for me. Then it became our time and our wish to make and have. It became a monumental moment in time for me to give you all of me and appreciate the small things in life as loving you went onto become an astronomical collection of wishes I have ever had. Now, it is simply a reminder of you. It will be there for me, and I can only wish one more to send you, one more time where you thought of me, too.

3:18PM                6.22.19          St. George, UT

I know it has not been easy for you. I know this will be one of the most difficult transitions for you, but just know no matter how heavy and grueling it gets, I will help you with the burden, with the ache, with whatever you are fucking going through or will come across your path. Even though we are not the same as we used to be and once were, your well being still means something deeply to me that I cannot explain based on what you did to me, but protecting you and the outcome you want, still matters to me. I have always wanted to help those I could because no one helped me as a child and it heals that part of me I thought was gone for good.

2:00PM 11.16.22 Texas

I wake up more surprised than the day before.

I have lived a hundred lives, yet, it is still a

mystery being here. It can be unsettling, but I

hope you are still here with me each time

my eyes find reason to remain open.

1:58PM
10.13.23
The Red Journal
No Name Saloon/Park City, UT


Love this fucking rust off of my heart,

my eyes, my burdened soul. Waking up

to morning on the windows, I talk to the light

and ask it to please be fucking kind and not

bend me to the ninety degree angle

I have been living.

2:25PM
10.13.23
The Red Journal
Atticus Coffee Shop
Park City, UT


May the reason you begin, never change.

And if it does, may it only be to increase

the value of yourself. Drink your days

of sun regularly and often.

12:31PM
10.14.23
The Red Journal
SLC

Break me out of my flesh, out of these

ordinary times our eyes are forced to take

in. Break my soul over the basking light,

and turn me into the colors running through

everything you love. Break my will to

leave should it ever come to that.

12:48PM
10.15.23
The Red Journal
SLC


Our purpose is not always known or made

to be figured out. We stress ourselves in

the action of discovering. Be patient with it

all. I have been trying to force things, love,

women, and everything else into my life to be

a part of it. But it will only find you when you

let go of everything you think you have

power over. Grief for anything is the

greatest teacher and counselor we

can have at our disposal.

3:34PM
10.15.23
The Red Journal
SLC

Dream your dreams.

Be relentless in all things

that bring you joy. You must

not forget, pain is temporary.

Bravery is forever.

4:06PM
10.15.23
The Red Journal
SLC


I have licked the light off of

windows and hands. Some broken.

Some scarred. And a few with bruises

that kept holding in and on too

tightly. I am a night-crawler, a slow

walker, a muted talker who begs too much.

4:53PM
10.16.23
The Red Journal
SLC

Between the hills, through the mountains,

and over the roads, you come to find

yourself thinking of those before you.

The settlers. The adventurers. The wild ones.

Those who found these places and what they

must have felt when they unearthed their souls

at the arrival, at the destination they had

no idea was awaiting them before they

set out to find everything they thought

they were missing and longing for.

12:18PM
10.17.23
The Eating Establishment
The Red Journal
Park City, UT


Wherever you find yourself today,

may the sun be shining on your face

and the love around you be enough to

get you through whatever you are facing today.

12:24PM
10.17.23
The Eating Establishment
The Red Journal
PArk City, UT


Through the trees, leaves all surrendered,

there is still a naked beauty about standing

before such poetry the earth has sprouted

and bloomed to allow those who seek

acceptance, to feel welcomed by it all,

by every piece of ravaged sign of life.

1:30PM
10.17.23
The Red Journal
Farm Trailhead, UT


Be only afraid of the moments you miss,

the moments gone unnoticed. We are all

desperately in search of meaning, purpose,

and drive. I hope when eighty finds me,

I will have love there beside me, holding

on dearly to the hands that walked it home

every night without needing to ask me to.

2:18PM
10.17.23
Cleveland St.
The Red Journal
SLC


Leaving a place you never wish to leave is

always a difficult circumstance to find

yourself in. Especially when you are going

back to an area, state, and home you do

not choose or wish to be a part of.

More slow dying, walking around a

blue track, waiting for something I

have no idea about to find me by not

being able to do nothing at all but exactly

that. This is not living at all. It is a repetitive

cycle of hoping to change what you cannot control.

7:07AM                    8.1.24                    Texas


My heart still knows your name and refuses to speak.

There is no end to this silence. I feel as though

it will be the main reason why my writing will

be my only language when it comes to

describing the love I need.

12:36PM                    5.5.24                    Texas

There will come a time when you may feel as though nothing you do is enough, that if you breathe too heavy your lungs will give up. You are meant for this life, this world, this experience of a soul living in a body. To be human, means to know loss, but it is a beautiful blessing to be able to feel anything at all when this world is based on numbing yourself entirely. Catch your dreams and hold on as tightly as you can. Do not throw or release any of them back into the abyss, because this will end, and our story depends on the souvenirs we deem worthy of our astute effort.

7:22PM                7.12.14                Texas

Before I met you, every day felt like I was drowning in

a place no one could find me. Since then, I have felt

like water, keeping ships afloat and making sure you

had a reason to jump from puddle to puddle, as if you

never forgot what being youthful meant.

6:28PM          6.11.24     Texas/RM116

Whenever I travel, it takes at least a few days for me to

gather my feelings. My thoughts are somewhere on the

road, a few hours behind me, and I wait until they catch

up with me. Until then, I am a human for a few hours

EACH BOOK THAT IS BOUGHT FROM MY WEBSITE WILL HAVE ITS OWN REASON HANDWRITTEN OUT ON THIS EXACT PAGE. THE REASONS ARE ENDLESS, JUST AS IS MY LOVE FOR THE STATE ITSELF AND EVERYTHING IT GAVE TO ME THEN AND NOW.

-------------------------------------------------------------------------

### <u>*WHY UTAH MEANS WHAT IT DOES TO ME*</u>:

www.ingramcontent.com/pod-product-compliance
Lightning Source LLC
Chambersburg PA
CBHW021119180726
47993CB00021B/3079